Frédéric Delalot

washingtonias and zoetropes 10

KDP Editions

© KDP Editions 2022
ISBN: 9798351682808 (printed book)
Copyright Standard Copyright License

1

We projected ourselves in these courses

It would be one of the worlds...

I rubbed shoulders with souls in love...

I wanted every hour...

Like the passion and the first moments

Several years later, everything seems far away

The path was coves, universe

Immensity of adventures...

At an exciting pace...

She was naked between our feelings.

Hugging in the hues...

Speed, with no other alternative...

Looks at the origin of our steps...

Illusions and even attractions...

In the festive second that came

I could see the French glow...

Pleasant hours...

Days of discovery and unknown

Bohemian outfits, transparent...

Night of joy at Le Lavandou...

We had run after desires...

Many universes by tinting them

The young wanderer...

Until nightfall...

Smiles on a doorstep

Innocuous roads that the sea calls for

We were playing to be ourselves...

Details, flying papers...

And I placed myself near the bays...

My memory recreated eras...

When everything was in slow motion...

Still to live the elusive moment

Another story or the same...

The perfect opportunity...

Where the night was just a simple night

Through the travel sheets...

Timepiece of a few dreams...

In the distance, sailboats...

That we hardly saw anymore

We projected ourselves in these courses

Phantasmagoric

Mediterranean...

Under a pine tree...

Night readings...

At twenty, getting drunk...

Between indecision and possibilities.

Together...

Bitterness and fullness...

Would rub shoulders, much later

Dose of reborn passion...

Beams of light...

Inside stones

Tiny, infinity...

From the global spirit...

It would be one of the worlds...

Possible, floated our emotions

Then our hasty lives...

And the years, with innocuous care.

A few photons...

The pale pink snow...

Impulses of feelings

Illusions...

By touches, eras...

Intertwined lives...

A laughing voice in Manhattan

Emotions, youth bonuses...

All the years that have passed...

Hypnotic state, from floor to floor

I rubbed shoulders with souls in love...

Energetic...

Passage, not even twenty years old

Where we had loved the splendor...

Penumbra illuminated by headlights

Unexpectedly...

Suspended loves, eternal air

I wanted every hour...

Perfect shapes and infinite cycles...

Going in the direction of a rediscovery

Candles in Bormes, Montreal...

Unusual penumbra of the reunion...

We hid in the middle of the evenings

Easy bodies, Europe...

It seems to me...

When we were younger...

Perhaps they had promised each other happiness.

Discreet, beings in their desires...

A timeless style...

Which was her own, quickly done...

We had gone to the edge of the world...

At the limit, joy that we hoped for stories

We had walked, happy together

A slow advance swallowed every distance

Outside, appeared every day...

As a sine qua non...

Like the passion and the first moments...

Maybe it was fun, after all...

Several years later, everything seems far away

In cahoots with time itself...

We rarely escape...

At the parade of the fourteenth...

The TGV had been delayed

I think...

Maybe not...

Playful look

Openness

On the world...

Temporary...

We had driven...

Completely...

Up to a house

Hidden...

Laughter, the pinnacle of youth...

All kinds of people, these sneaks...

Had a perfume, and she had undressed

She passed naked from room to room...

Red lounge, fountains, it was easy...

The path was coves, erotic universe

Became look and acceptance to be...

Huge slate, the bodies mixed

The world continued to be ardent...

Comforting passion...

Blinds half closed...

Through the millennia

Ultimate oceans...

Or Paris, I don't know anymore...

There was in the voyeur space

Her desires...

And the planets...

The immensity of the adventures...

She was in front of us, going up...

A narrow staircase, magical whispers

Captives of rockeries...

The lights were changing...

Our transgressions, races of this time

Which inhabited me to infinity...

Recognized words, snippets...

Happiness on the heights of Florence...

I wouldn't have changed the crazy passion...

Nor meals without waves, orgasm bodies

The world was dissipating and the time came...

Evenings that followed one another...

At an exciting pace...

Across empires...

Emotions, youth bonuses

Like this...

Like impossible things

That we had already expected

In the rain...

She was naked between our feelings...

Long rhythms in the street...

Other generations, other hopes

There were only magic trees left

And that totality...

We each had an occupation

And the car was driving...

We were taking us back to the hotel...

Beauties, waves.

Every night, almost every night...

Years, worlds, then...

Created parentheses...

Slowed down the time in the party

Extravagant...

And she confided in the glow...

There was a long time ago, without the race

Look, feeling, impression...

Hugging in the hues...

Cream, beige, sleep...

In each era its adventures

At dawn, promise of reflections...

Imaginations and unforgettable abandonments...

There were our looks and a fleeting feeling

We finished a bottle of gin...

Instinctive attractions, mysterious curiosities...

Speed, with no other alternative...

When changing meant almost nothing...

You know, the memories had diluted...

Attic hotel room, with unforgettable character

So many hopes...

Festive foliage...

Leaning mezzanine

On the large hall...

Macadam and chocolate cookies

We, our cat, looked at the trees...

The scenes, in the distance, of the sailboats...

That we hardly saw anymore...

Waiting positions...

As we approached

Over there...

From the beginning...

Looks at the origin of our steps

I remembered...

We would continue to invent ourselves

See you again...

While away the hours...

However long I stay...

Next to it, others were resting

Instant, feeling drunk...

As at the hidden source...

Distant, from our dreams...

Nothing more than easy postures

Instinctive, and the moment...

Loving life for you and me...

Illusions and even attractions

Ardor in low sofas

First gold dust...

Transient appearance...

Chanted lyrics...

From a song...

They were picking up leaves

Spheres, whirling...

Until dawn...

On active days...

Like cyborgs...

Comings from which we did not know from where

Unexpectedly, during this season...

The cool wind made things take things back

In the festive second that came...

In the center of the remote fortifications...

Very far...

Bright...

Part of a change

Larger...

She would think of islands of dreams

Images of yesteryear, chipped ...

Precious moments...

I found in the intonations...

So many pure instincts, at the end of a span of time

In a hooded aviator's jacket...

I perceived the French glow

Sleeping fields...

Suburbs...

Rusty convoys...

Weekend...

I was passing on Sainte-Catherine

Ally of the cities, probably...

Visitor...

Pleasant hours

At the end of the week...

I was getting involved...

In the present...

They had to capture reality

Bastille, Montmartre, Montreal...

We had met again one evening...

Deciduous trees...

There was no hour...

Only to wait...

To be against each other

Space of significant traces...

Eminently following things...

View of the activity of the dancefloor...

Days of discovery and unknown

Sculptures of the apartments...

Virgins of all decoration...

In blue Mazda, other years...

Between the reeds, as far as Spain

Constantly rejuvenated...

My own story...

Sucked us in, repetitions

From chapters already written...

From their bodies, rides...

Years passed...

There, it would be the day before the crowds

Bohemian outfits, transparent

Passengers, attractive...

Got drunk day and night...

And eras had been lived...

Holographic spheres...

The greenery mixed with the stones of yesteryear.

The fresh wind soothed...

Classic surroundings

They were like that

As an ambition...

Garden...

Around the Moon...

Encompassing almost all

Orders from the planet...

Transis of embraces...

Marine...

And the future had always been there

Night of joy at Le Lavandou...

On the ground of tiny elegance...

Our desires, the attraction of our bodies

Life at the heart of the spheres...

We had run after desires...

There was a party, glimmers

Bohemian or hippie dresses

Continuation of the crazy life...

Long hours...

And we even liked things...

Unfinished, glows in the trees...

Evenings, nights towards Place Blanche

At dawn, like lovers...

Volutes, and the friends of yesteryear...

Pampered streets, nocturnal cobblestones...

Buildings, more towers...

I was getting back on the road.

Live from New York...

An unprecedented Sun...

Many universes by tinting them

Instinctive curves

Forever...

Verbatim...

Continuing...

The race...

Along the arches.

Recovering diamonds

Right on the street...

Between the slats...

Blinds, yellowed...

The space freeing up flow...

I remember photographs

A few months...

Of a shared solitude...

One hundred years of slow writing

The young wanderer...

Memory of countries...

Billions of emphases...

Sincerity revealed...

At the time of facets

Gold coins...

I was far away, that's all

Pedestrian streets...

Until nightfall

Hacienda...

Coincidences...

And I saw her...

That year...

At night...

Chance dreams on the pontoon

Slight shortcuts of departures...

Floats, landscapes, here and there

Much further south...

Bohemians from elsewhere...

Chance, as they say...

A murky dream...

The staircase wound in eras

Smiles on a doorstep

A few laps...

Like this...

The same places...

Often, wood from Spain

Saturated with vials...

Season of contrasts...

In a pile of sheets...

There was this whole story

Erotic distance...

Innocuous roads that the sea calls for...

I clung to flying papers...

Captivated by lack of sleep...

At this time of noctilucent clouds

Unique and unknown, in the middle of the posters

A story of emotions and frolics...

Overcoming the whirlwind of Architecture...

Centuries had passed...

Multitude of attractions...

Magnetic paths...

Weekend, icy wind...

We played to be ourselves

As for a caressing party

Crossing borders...

Without restraint, years passed

In a split second...

Eternal...

And curious...

Friends of the party

In a courtyard...

Interior...

In a neighborhood

In a latitude

Indian...

Sensual certainties...

Until nightfall

Details, flying papers...

Lonely, perhaps...

There were dwarves...

From gardens, that year

Shows...

Electro music...

The park pond was frozen.

And I placed myself near the bays

In order to observe the surroundings...

And what they had become...

Oasis of the building...

Slow street and larger squares

Near the huge cacti...

We were naked...

Inside the terminals...

From my imagination...

Myths of youth

Joys listed...

Infinite mirages...

Over there...

World...

And habits

Would have changed

In cafes, in the city...

And my gaze hovered...

My memory recreated eras

Emotions...

Relaxing...

Uninhibited...

Pleasant juxtapositions

Staging...

Succulents, tropical...

Lolailolaolailolai...

At night, during dream hours...

Nights in white satin, never reaching the end...

12

Ah! there were trees...

When everything was in slow motion...

Thirst to know the easy look

The balm, the alcoves...

There had been mixtures

Hours of enthusiasm...

Senseless caresses...

Mistresses of time

And travel...

It is a hamlet lost under the stars...

Forgotten the laughter of harvest nights...

And turned on the television sets...

Unfinished terraces, distant paths

The trips, the flavors of the pies...

We were getting there...

Still to live the elusive moment

Dressed, undressed...

Plots of eternity...

On the road, this time...

All these times from other eras

Moments of enthusiasm, attractions...

Exaggerated...

Pleasant relationships

Quiet enjoyment

Advances...

Endless...

Feeling an emotion

And we wanted...

Occasionally...

My friends were arriving

Skateboarding...

Inkjet...

On translucent canvas

Where we would invent ourselves...

More reasons to be...

Another story or the same...

Give me a life... A tomorrow to today...

13

By swivelling...

They generated effects

The unfolding...

The perfect opportunity...

Surreptitiously next page

In the course of things...

No hours, this time

Just realities...

Temporal...

Where the night was just a simple night

As if out of the universe, snowy evenings

We consulted with you the archives...

The television served as a multicolored lamp

Diminished our consciousness...

Palm trees, flamingos...

And I didn't get out of the imagination...

Memories on the horizon, floating in front of me

Then we left the Old

We were in the air of the streets...

Hopes of transient feelings

Ideas for the future...

Tall trees and parks...

We were Ferris wheel...

Bright, hallucinogenic...

Through travel sheets

For a moment...

The tram had taken us down...

Near the Lez, state-of-the-art turrets

Trees of the time and streets around...

Tiny headphones

Translucent...

Prime youth...

There was music

Human being...

Who let himself be heard

At dawn...

Facing the sea...

14

Lying down and looking at the horizon...

I had remembered a long vacation

Gleaming slopes in the shape of banks...

Which no one is satisfied with...

Timepiece of a few dreams

How many possible moments...

Talk Talk or Tears for Fears

The day had run away...

At the bar of the new town...

I could see the trees

Black, leaning...

From the road...

Transgressions...

Races...

There were parties...

Fairgrounds, attractions

To the South...

Mopeds

Masquerades

Complex

To be identified...

A circle included us...

Described a figure...

In space and time

I overlooked the summer...

Other nights, finally...

She looked like slender beings...

Martian colonies...

Summer had the rhythm of our embraces

Maybe just that...

We would continue...

He was repeating this sentence to me

Excerpted from I didn't know where

When his mind wandered

I remembered it at the time

While we were talking...

Unreason, nonchalance, later.

New things, written in the making...

Quiet progress, unfulfillments...

A little cider, maple syrup maybe

We hurried not to regret anything...

Walking other streets, warming up

More, imperishable summits...

Thus, from the top of our hopes...

There were many outstanding expectations

Many ways...

Film of the days

Sequences, in serious joy...

Inexhaustible circles...

We were heading into the moment

White pages with ease

Messengers from other worlds

We dreamed of being real...

Like in a game...

We had followed a country road

A path together, and there were those days

At first, maybe at first...

Imperceptible sensation, here is the time...

As if the years had not passed

And on moons or satellites...

We dreamed of snowy evenings...

We were getting closer to the present...

Maple syrup like that...

On pancakes with fruits from the fields

A series of narrations, surroundings...

In the center of a proscenium...

I could see a little bit of the River and the roads

In the distance, the continual comings and goings...

Other years, harms outside...

Light of the centuries, inside...

Exoplanet...

Billions of emphases...

Until nightfall...

The Ferris wheel was turning pink.

Then blue, white, red...

Gradually multicolored

All this mingled with winter

Retrospective...

Random T-shirts

And sleepless nights...

Pictured life from yesterday...

Pictured life, pictured life...

Longing for the sun you will come...

To the island many miles away from home

A large box of chocolates...

Through the streets and foliage...

We were looking at the past...

Uninhibited America

Pleasures, drifts...

Forgetting in the horizon

Senses...

Each round lasted...

A thousand days and a thousand nights...

From the depths of the exciting ages...

The evening enveloped the scenery with snow.

Emeralds of eternity...

On the ochre sand beaches

Under the blue sky then purple

And there were mirages...

Images, infinite energy...

Allures without constraints...

And there were projections

Artistic, streets...

I remembered the creeks

Affable seductions...

In some youth...

Stories, sublimated images

Grandmaster Flash and the Furious Five...

I remember those slammed doors...

I was only traveling, at the dawn of the rides

From the South, one summer, road of other years...

17

I would have spent whole evenings

In art galleries...

Abandoned to daydreaming...

Everywhere, like skylights...

The wind carried our desires away...

Like these triumphs of the ephemeral

Waiting for an exceptional dawn

The tram had taken us down

Near the Lez...

Prime youth...

Nothing erotic...

Do we know what...

Before you hit the road

To the South...

The signs of the countryside...

Asleep our surroundings...

Everything was different, we were young

There had been snow

Room in the air...

Stone walls...

Between the trees...

I saw the emerging glows again...

We were going back in time...

I was waiting with the streets dotted around

How many possible moments...

First promises of euphoria...

Enthusiastic faces, there was a momentum...

A thousand years from here, beams of light

Sometimes we stayed on the sand...

Oasis, yellow dress...

Under an arch...

Coherence...

From a distant expectation

Irresistible looks...

In the great century that was coming...

I was rediscovering old emotions

Pleasant drunkenness...

18

Without the sea, since such curves do not last

In the past, appointments, festivities...

The road was pristine, astonishing...

Attempted wanderings...

So many peaks, so many euphorias

At the amaranth binding...

To the crazy terraces...

Debonair attitudes, born in the past

Memory of the insurmountable dream.

Which will be ours, forever, disproportionate seaside ...

Loves, the sky is big, you have to believe in the light

It seemed that everything was an interlude...

We were exploring alchemical avenues...

That voice from another era that whispers...

I wanted to take a tour...

It was to find our shore, by chance...

Timepiece of a few dreams, this latitude

Boat masts, during student margins

From orange terraces to tram bends

Winding breaks...

To get some fresh air for years, some havens...

Pagoda, palm trees...

The Mediterranean extended to wildlife...

Eucalyptus, around protected ferns...

And the nights were short, we hurried

I remembered the first night

Mind-blowing freedom...

And a little more...

Mazes of the stone village...

Overlooking progress...

Transparent vials of a summer sky

Memory of pleasures...

Which mastered illusions...

There are many stories...

And evenings where we believe

We were those dreams...

Far from the world...

19

So we quenched our thirst...

In the delectable space, filled with pignes...

Purple, we arrived through a wise labyrinth

At the stopover, the rasades...

Night scenes...

From the peninsula to desires

The air of the ocean, far away...

I remembered those moments...

Rest of the vineyards of Lavandou.

Water lilies, twigs...

Flights, lapping...

It was a very aerial moment

What we were hoping for...

The main thing is still happening now

To the shudder of the ephemeral...

There had been frames...

The interior space revealed itself at rest...

Far from the world...

We had relaxed...

It is that we had established many parenthesis

Ignoring the routine...

Memories of trips...

Tourist compartment...

Everything remembers...

The blank page was rushing

To the Sailing School...

The pond of Pissevaches

In its purest form...

Pleasant flexibility...

One night...

Previous years

Perfect harmonies...

That's the time...

A Hindu air...

Camouflaged...

Hoping to be entertained

Strange sky of forces...

20

Chandeliers before...

These ideas, these promises

This quest...

In the light...

At night...

Creates the unforgettable

We were driving towards the coast...

The future, this time...

Inviting, offered themselves to us.

I was hoping for a merger...

Era of improvisations...

Invisible, under the sheets...

Close to that of light

Behind translucent doors

Silhouettes, resting...

Brief agreements...

Slopes of ecstasy...

We interfered

Slammed doors...

Incarnations of the nights...

At the bottom of a park...

I remembered that I had been another

I was erasing the numbers...

We would create beings...

The night sparkled...

Possible agreements

From the road...

At dawn...

Crossings...

As in a thesis...

Arid happiness, memories

On the horizon...

Giants of the future...

And there was music

Truces...

Panoramas...

Nights...

21

And so was the world

Desire for freedom...

Season...

Ah! in the distance...

Horses of light, splendid...

We were going through intoxicating parks

Expectation of the anchor

Nothing happens...

The word is strong...

Taste of a rhythm

Meanders...

From forecourt...

One night...

Previous years

Oceanic canvases...

Nudity...

Frightening...

There you go...

A Hindu air

Titanic...

Sculptures...

In the hope of loving

Bareback...

Drizzle...

Promises...

This quest...

At dawn...

Sometimes...

Creates the unforgettable

Under a vault...

Let us watch

Naked...

Era of mixtures

Invisible...

Out of bounds...

Behind doors

Translucent...

22

Silhouettes...

We were born

For a moment

We interfered

High lunches...

Raw, waltzing...

Castle in the storm

The splendor would last, turns

Ink of the dunes...

There at the cadences...

Endorsements...

At dawn...

As in a thesis

Arid happiness...

Memorabilia...

Clear waves...

Escaped images

Packing...

Thought that is given...

Towards the center of time

Sea air...

Returning from ancient tunes

And winter was coming back...

Favorite topics...

Cosmos...

Blinds...

Lighting ramps...

Red stones and bricks

All the way to the border...

Disguised...

Between branches

Sunset...

Cafés...

Travel courier...

Distant paths...

I remembered the look of bridges

To be that dream...

23

And rue des Taillandiers

The moorings...

Crossing, bends...

The road...

Quick patterns...

Car to drive

Meeting place

I remembered...

With a speed...

Bastions of yesterday...
We walked in the streets
There were words...
In the unknown...

Ornaments, black coffee...
From La Loco to the Baths
Returning from a bazaar
Interlude...

Moment of indifference
Moments...
Joyful evening...
We were sleeping...

I was going up a flight of stairs

Real rapprochement...

Youth...

Flush with the coast...

The Space of the Night

Escape from nothingness...

Seasons...

Fast surface...

She would be waiting for me...

Invincible...

Since dawn...

On the roof terrace

Appointment...

Music of the cities...

Time was loving...

We had to change the energy.

24

Very far...

Nothing was happening

Slow day trotting

With friends...

Crossing paths in the street...

There were unreal worlds

Old novels

Old-fashioned tags

Decades...

With other archives...

Minishort in pink sequins...

Red lights...

Projects, boil in the thirties

Long sequence, images...

Shapes, moments...

Energy recharged curves

Near the porch of a manor house...

Summers, springs...

In the warmth of the musicians

Between the currents...

From La Clape, full moon...

We were levitating...

Mosaic of temptations...

Allies...

The lanterns dazzled us

While years had passed

Nonchalance, just a moment...

A thousand pages...

Intermittency...

And birds flew away

Unlikely...

Letters I've written...

Never meaning to send...

Did we know it then

The future was anchored...

Still the exaltation...

I remembered...

25

I stared at the sky...

Underground corridor...

Even for a short time

Sunny...

Lives...

And things

Alcohols...

Unique destiny...

Turquoise tunic.

Very short...

Chance brushing

Secret corners...

Yesterday residents...

Dreamers by the way

Full of doors...

Calm snow...

Photographs...

Landscape...

From a Peloponnese

From a tower...

Apache...

Debauchery of energy...

Behind the ramparts

Between the trees...

Insatiable happiness

Latitude, worry-free evening...

The opposite of things

Desire to be reborn...

Between the eyes of the trees...

Under the palm trees...

And the villas...

Appearances...

We had this path

They had recovered

Flight...

Indifference...

Reassuring...

26

Strength of a procession

Parsimony...

Contrasts...

Like maps...

Like this...

Column of light

Asian...

Galaxies would merge

Epilogue...

The intense story of a yesterday...

Planets were engines

In these places...

Our attractions...

Appearances...

Subtle...

Spaces...

Running after the moment

The road to Paris...

By taking the time

Waves, episodes

Change scenery.

Lightness...

In the moment

Colours...

Turrets...

Unmissable...

Oblique pleasures

All logic...

At the heart of the senses...

The world went on...

Confusing...

There was a shortcut

Alternative...

Osmosis fluid...

By a transversal era

Mezzanines...

Lofts...

27

Youth...

I gave myself time

To undertake...

Quiet power...

Particles in space

Magnetic nights...

Dreams...

From the tunnel escaped

The vehicles...

Our pride is not adorned with any artifice

You were strolling, helicopters flashing...

We hurried to hug each other...

Green gardens of my summers...

In light of attitudes...

These screens were watering us

Freedom, through the city...

Artistic, promises...

The pleasant air, the tours...

We were looking at each other...

In the unhooked mirrors...

Dawn and evening terminals.

Three silver dolphins on an azure field

Automatic rhythms...

Like cars...

That we have...

Illusion of a time

Coat of reality...

Measurable...

Architecture...

Luxurious moments...

At the frontiers of the seconds

Temporary distances...

Days...

Freedoms, innocuous races

Maverick crowds...

Half an hour in front of you

Bubbles or moments.

28

Finish the night...

And we even liked it

Unfinished things...

We remembered

Times gone by...

Landscapes...

On the beaches of ochre sand...

Under the blue and then purple sky...

We were those dreams, so to speak.

Remembrance of the mystery

Silhouettes...

Psyches...

Blank page...

And winter was coming back...

Even for a short time

Near the porch...

From a manor house...

All logic...

Period of pace...

Sudden pleasures...

Many fall asleep.

Immensity...

For an outside eye

She wanted more...

Under the fanfares...

Sensual...

Yews and lilacs...

Border...

From the planet

Cliffs...

From the ocean...

In the wave...

Continuity...

Influence...

Human being...

Beaches...

Grains of sand.

29

Nascent human

It comes from far away...

Escaping...

In bohemians...

Invited a memory...

There was in the evening the perfume

Possible things

The old town...

Was relaxing...

Beginnings...

You were naked...

Infinite freedoms...

The century was long

Passing strangers dancing

Undressed...

We talked...

With nomads...

We'd see you again...

Attracted...

Young adults from ancient times

Happiness, adventure...

Overhanging...

Spray bays

Fog...

From an era...

A very long time ago

Caresses...

Thought...

Meeting...

Multiple...

In the park

Images...

I lived in

Occasionally...

Near the caravans...

Gravitation, passages

Elegance...

And we had peace

Multiple colors

Atmosphere...

Decoration of shelves...

Blissful retreat...

Somewhere in July

Nothing else...

That we thought they were random

Hours from the coast.

Elastic present...

The excitement...

Departures...

Attention chapardeuse

Within this area...

When I was twenty years old

Bird flights...

Tough dreams...

Hopes...

At the same time

I remember

With this doubt...

Booklets, dominating a Zen court

Regular artifact scenes...

We need parentheses

Diabolos, a remote era...

Branches that are captured

As you look around...

Timeless clothes...

And she will look the same

Lightness...

Drifts...

For smoother empires

Pine cones...

Didn't we hear...

The notes that we touch ...

Only, new days...

To the pose of slow suggestions.

© KDP Editions 2022
ISBN: 9798351682808 (printed book)
Copyright Standard Copyright License

www.ingramcontent.com/pod-product-compliance
Lightning Source LLC
Chambersburg PA
CBHW071933120726

48001CB00005B/1956